797.3   Abdo, Kenny
ABD   Windsurfing

ACTION SPORTS

WINDSURFING

KENNY ABDO

abdopublishing.com

Published by Abdo Zoom, a division of ABDO, P.O. Box 398166, Minneapolis, Minnesota 55439. Copyright © 2018 by Abdo Consulting Group, Inc. International copyrights reserved in all countries. No part of this book may be reproduced in any form without written permission from the publisher.

Printed in the United States of America, North Mankato, Minnesota.
092017
012018

THIS BOOK CONTAINS RECYCLED MATERIALS

Photo Credits: Alamy, AP Images, iStock, Shutterstock
Production Contributors: Kenny Abdo, Jennie Forsberg, Grace Hansen
Design Contributors: Dorothy Toth, Neil Klinepier

Publisher's Cataloging-in-Publication Data

Names: Abdo, Kenny, author.
Title: Windsurfing / by Kenny Abdo.
Description: Minneapolis, Minnesota: Abdo Zoom, 2018. | Series: Action sports |
    Includes online resource and index.
Identifiers: LCCN 2017939268 | ISBN 9781532120978 (lib.bdg.) |
    ISBN 9781532122095 (ebook) | ISBN 9781532122651 (Read-to-Me ebook)
Subjects: LCSH: Windsurfing--Juvenile literature. | Water Sports--Juvenile
    literature. | Extreme Sports—Juvenile literature.
Classification: DDC 797.33--dc23
LC record available at https://lccn.loc.gov/2017939268

TABLE OF CONTENTS

WINDSURFING

Windsurfing is a **watersport** that uses a light board and **sail**. It combines parts of both sailing and surfing.

Windsurfers stand on a board and move a **sail**. They use the wind and waves to glide on the water.

TYPES

A **sailor** and a surfer created the sport in the United States during the 1960s. It became a popular sport in the 1970s.

Windsurf boards are all similar in length. But they have different weights and widths for certain skill levels.

There are many kinds of boards for different types of windsurfing. These include freeride, slalom, wave, and speed windsurfing.

Boards used for **racing** and wave are usually very light.

COMPETITION

Modern windsurfing **competitions** are held throughout the world.

Freestyle and Wave are judged contests. The **sailor** with the best skill and variety wins.

The sport has been an **Olympic** event since 1984. Olympic windsurfers use the same 'One Design' boards that allow **racing** in many **sailing** conditions.

GLOSSARY

competition – an event where people compete in a skill.

Olympics – the biggest sporting event in the world that is divided into summer and winter games.

race – a competition of speed.

sail – a piece of material that catches wind and pushes a boat or board.

sailor - a person who goes sailing as a sport or recreation.

slalom - high-speed race where sailors navigate around floating beams.

watersport – any sport played in or on water.

ONLINE RESOURCES

Booklinks
NONFICTION NETWORK
FREE! ONLINE NONFICTION RESOURCES

To learn more about windsurfing, please visit abdobooklinks.com. These links are routinely monitored and updated to provide the most current information available.

INDEX